POPULAR SOLOS
for Young Singers

Popular
SOLOS

ISBN 978-0-7935-3444-9

HAL•LEONARD®
CORPORATION

7777 W. BLUEMOUND RD. P.O. BOX 13819 MILWAUKEE, WI 53213

Visit Hal Leonard Online at
www.halleonard.com

CONTENTS

The Bare Necessities

from Walt Disney's THE JUNGLE BOOK

Words and Music by
TERRY GILKYSON

Look for the bare ne - ces - si - ties, the sim - ple bare ne -

ces - si - ties, __ for - get a - bout your wor - ries and your strife. I mean the

bare ne - ces - si - ties __ or Moth - er Na - ture's re - ci - pes __ that bring the bare ne -

Be Kind to Your Parents

from FANNY

Words and Music by
HAROLD ROME

Bibbidi-Bobbidi-Boo
(The Magic Song)
from Walt Disney's CINDERELLA

Words by JERRY LIVINGSTON
Music by MACK DAVID and AL HOFFMAN

The Ballad of Davy Crockett

from Walt Disney's DAVY CROCKETT – KING OF THE WILD FRONTIER

Words by TOM BLACKBURN
Music by GEORGE BRUNS

Only verses 1, 2 and 18 are recorded on the accompaniment CD.

14

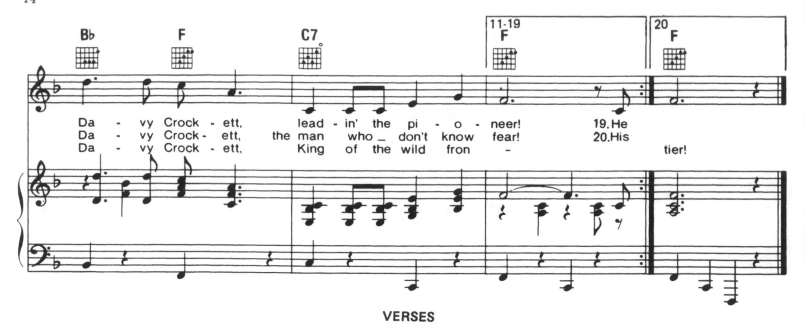

Da - vy Crock - ett, lead - in' the pi - o - neer!   19.He
Da - vy Crock - ett, the man who don't know fear!   20.His
Da - vy Crock - ett, King of the wild fron - tier!

VERSES

4.
Andy Jackson is our gen'ral's name,
His reg'lar soldiers we'll put to shame,
Them redskin varmints us Volunteers'll tame,
'Cause we got the guns with the sure-fire aim.
Davy — Davy Crockett,
The champion of us all!

5.
Headed back to war from the ol' home place,
But Red Stick was leadin' a merry chase,
Fightin' an' burnin' at a devil's pace
South to the swamps on the Florida Trace.
Davy — Davy Crockett,
Trackin' the redskins down!

6.
Fought single-handed through the Injun War
Till the Creeks was whipped an' peace was in store,
An' while he was handlin' this risky chore,
Made hisself a legend for evermore.
Davy — Davy Crockett,
King of the wild frontier!

7.
He give his word an' he give his hand
That his Injun friends could keep their land,
An' the rest of his life he took the stand
That justice was due every redskin band.
Davy — Davy Crockett,
Holdin' his promise dear!

8.
Home fer the winter with his family,
Happy as squirrels in the ol' gum tree,
Bein' the father he wanted to be,
Close to his boys as the pod an' the pea.
Davy — Davy Crockett,
Holdin' his young 'uns dear!

9.
But the ice went out an' the warm winds came
An' the meltin' snow showed tracks of game,
An' the flowers of Spring filled the woods with flame,
An' all of a sudden life got too tame.
Davy — Davy Crockett,
Headin' on West again!

10.
Off through the woods we're riding' along,
Makin' up yarns an' singin' a song,
He's ringy as a b'ar an' twict as strong,
An' knows he's right 'cause he ain't often wrong.
Davy — Davy Crockett,
The man who don't know fear!

11.
Lookin' fer a place where the air smells clean,
Where the trees is tall an' the grass is green,
Where the fish is fat in an untouched stream,
An' the teemin' woods is a hunter's dream.
Davy — Davy Crockett,
Lookin' fer Paradise!

12.
Now he'd lost his love an' his grief was gall,
In his heart he wanted to leave it all,
An' lose himself in the forests tall,
But he answered instead his country's call.
Davy — Davy Crockett,
Beginnin' his campaign!

13.
Needin' his help they didn't vote blind,
They put in Davy 'cause he was their kind,
Sent up to Nashville the best they could find,
A fightin' spirit an' a thinkin' mind.
Davy — Davy Crockett,
Choice of the whole frontier!

14.
The votes were counted an' he won hands down,
So they sent him off to Washin'ton town
With his best dress suit still his buckskins brown,
A livin' legend of growin' renown.
Davy — Davy Crockett,
The Canebrake Congressman!

15.
He went off to Congress an' served a spell,
Fixin' up the Gover'ment an' laws as well,
Took over Washin'ton so we heered tell
An' patched up the crack in the Liberty Bell.
Davy — Davy Crockett,
Seein' his duty clear!

16.
Him an' his jokes travelled all through the land,
An' his speeches made him friends to beat the band,
His politickin' was their favorite brand
An' everyone wanted to shake his hand.
Davy — Davy Crockett,
Helpin' his legend grow!

17.
He knew when he spoke he sounded the knell
Of his hopes for White House an' fame as well,
But he spoke out strong so hist'ry books tell
An patched up the crack in the Liberty Bell.
Davy — Davy Crockett,
Seein' his duty clear!

Candle on the Water

from Walt Disney's PETE'S DRAGON

Words and Music by AL KASHA
and JOEL HIRSCHHORN

I'll be your can-dle on the wa-ter, my love for you will al-ways burn.
I'll be your can-dle on the wa-ter 'til ev-'ry wave is warm and bright.

I know you're lost and drift-ing, but the clouds are lift-ing.
My soul is there be-side you, let this can-dle guide you;

Don't give up; you have some-where to turn.
soon you'll see a gold-en stream of light.

The Chipmunk Song

Words and Music by
ROSS BAGDASARIAN

Close Every Door

from JOSEPH AND THE AMAZING TECHNICOLOR DREAMCOAT

Lyrics by TIM RICE
Music by ANDREW LLOYD WEBBER

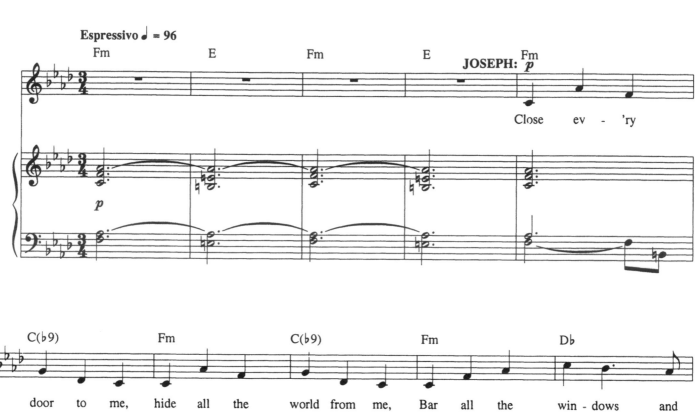

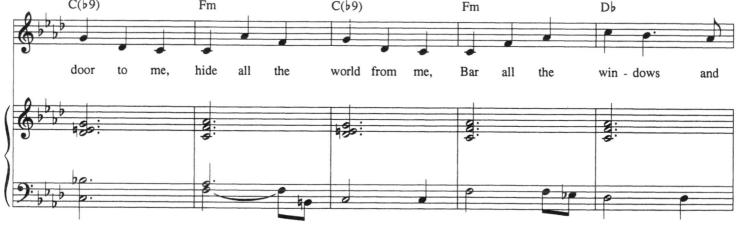

lone, For I know I shall find my own peace of mind, For

I have been prom-ised a land of my own.

Just give me a num-ber in-stead of my

Count Your Blessings Instead of Sheep

from The Motion Picture Irving Berlin's WHITE CHRISTMAS

Words and Music by
IRVING BERLIN

Dream for Your Inspiration

from THE MUPPETS TAKE MANHATTAN

By SCOTT BROWNLEE

I used to get to feel-ing so down heart-ed.
I used to think that I was noth-ing spe - cial,
So if you think that you are me-di - o - cre,

I used to e - ven hate the
that I was just an-oth-er
and ev-'ry-thing you do is

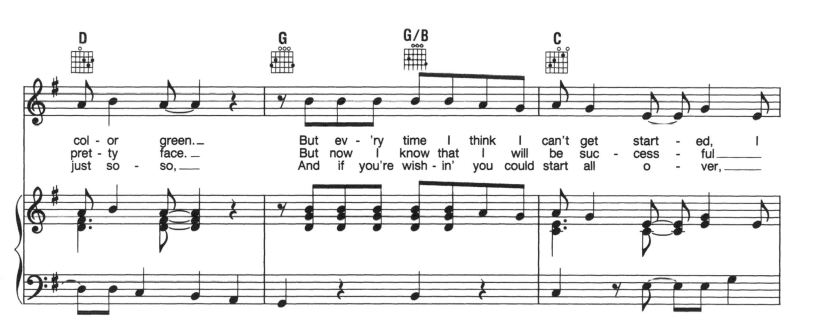

col - or green.__
pret - ty face.__
just so - so,__

But ev-'ry time I think I can't get start - ed, I
But now I know that I will be suc-cess - ful
And if you're wish-in' you could start all o - ver,

think of all my dreams and then I'm right back on the beam. You've got to
if I al-ways do just what I real - ly want to do. You've got to
stop and re-al - ize you've got your dreams and you'll be fine. You've got to

dream   for your
dream   of your

Getting Tall

from NINE

Words and Music by
MAURY YESTON

If Momma Was Married

from GYPSY

Words by STEPHEN SONDHEIM
Music by JULE STYNE

JUNE:

Mom-ma was mar-ried. If Mom-ma was mar-ried, I'd jump in the air And give all my toe-shoes to you. I'd get all these hair-rib-bons out of my hair And once and for all I'd get Mom-ma out too. If Mom-ma was

In My Own Little Corner

from CINDERELLA

Lyrics by OSCAR HAMMERSTEIN II
Music by RICHARD RODGERS

The repeat of the refrain is not recorded on the accompaniment CD.

On the Good Ship Lollipop

from BRIGHT EYES

Words and Music by SIDNEY CLARE
and RICHARD A. WHITING

On the good ship — lol - li - pop, — It's a sweet trip — to a

can - dy shop, — Where bon - bons play _____ on the sun - ny beach of

pep - per - mint bay. _____ Lem - on - ade stands —

The Rainbow Connection

from THE MUPPET MOVIE

Words and Music by PAUL WILLIAMS
and KENNETH L. ASCHER

Rubber Duckie
from SESAME STREET

Words and Music by
JEFFREY MOSS

Saying Goodbye

from THE MUPPETS TAKE MANHATTAN

By JEFF MOSS

The repeat is not recorded on the accompaniment CD.

Side by Side

Words and Music by
HARRY WOODS

Moderately

See that sun ___ in the morn - ing
We're all hunt - ing for some - thing

peek - ing o - ver the hill   I'll bet you're sure ___ it al - ways has ___ and
some-thing we ___ don't know what.   'Cause none of us ___ are sa - tis - fied ___ with

sure it al - ways will.   That's how I feel a - bout some - one   how
things we know we've got.   We all for - get a - bout moon - light   as

The repeat is not recorded on the accompaniment CD.

Sing
from SESAME STREET

Words and Music by
JOE RAPOSO

Moderately

A Spoonful of Sugar

from Walt Disney's MARY POPPINS

Words and Music by
RICHARD M. SHERMAN
and ROBERT B. SHERMAN

*Only two verses are recorded
on the accompaniment CD.*

Supercalifragilisticexpialidocious

from Walt Disney's MARY POPPINS

Words and Music by RICHARD M. SHERMAN
and ROBERT B. SHERMAN

MARY POPPINS

Sup - er - cal - i - frag - il - is - tic - ex - pi - al - i - do - cious!

E - ven though the sound of it is some - thing quite a - tro - cious,

If you say it loud e - nough, you'll al - ways sound pre - co - cious.

Waitin' for the Light to Shine

from BIG RIVER

Words and Music by
ROGER MILLER

Zip-A-Dee-Doo-Dah

from Walt Disney's SONG OF THE SOUTH

Words by RAY GILBERT
Music by ALLIE WRUBEL

MUSICAL THEATRE COLLECTIONS FOR SINGERS

Best of Broadway

Duet arrangements of theatre songs for soprano and baritone. Contains: All at Once You Love Her • Climb Ev'ry Mountain • Getting to Know You* • I Whistle a Happy Tune* • It Might as Well Be Spring • It's a Grand Night For Singing • Memory • My Favorite Things • Oh, What a Beautiful Mornin'* • People Will Say We're in Love • Sunrise, Sunset • The Sound of Music.

00312032 Vocal Duets $14.99

Broadway Classics

VOCAL SHEET MUSIC SERIES This exciting series for singers features authentic piano accompaniments and custom guitar chord diagrams, tailored to each song's unique chord progressions and designed to provide realistic support. Each volume includes dozens of songs from legendary Broadway productions.

00256670 Women's Edition (25 songs) $19.99
00256666 Men's Edition (37 songs) $19.99

The Broadway Ingénue

A wonderfully diverse collection of comedy songs, character songs, Vaudeville numbers, dramatic songs, and ballads for the actor who sings. A perfect resource for finding an audition piece or specialty number. Two editions, one for women and one for men, with a completely different selection of over 50 songs in each.

00000386 Soprano Book Only $24.99
00001017 Soprano Book/Online Audio $34.99

Contemporary Broadway Vocal Duets

This fabulous collection for women theatre singers includes piano/vocal arrangements in appropriately low belting keys of 38 songs to keep audiences laughing: Adelaide's Lament • Always a Bridesmaid • Dance: Ten; Looks: Three • Diamonds Are a Girl's Best Friend • Don't Call Me Trailer Trash • A Guy What Takes His Time • It Ain't Etiquette • Take Back Your Mink • Why Do the Wrong People Travel? • You Can't Get a Man with a Gun • more.

00125416 .... $22.99

Contemporary Theatre Songs

These collections of songs from the 21st century feature 33-37 songs per volume, with songs in original keys only, and a different song list for each voice type, with plot notes. Includes songs from Broadway, Off-Broadway and Off-Off Broadway.

00191892 Soprano $24.99
00191893 Mezzo-Soprano/Belter $24.99
00191894 Tenor $24.99
00191895 Baritone/Bass.................................... $24.99

First Book of Broadway Solos

These collections of songs from the 21st century feature 33-37 songs per volume, with songs in original keys only, and a different song list for each voice type, with plot notes. Includes songs from Broadway, Off-Broadway and Off-Off Broadway.

00740081 Soprano Book Only $17.99
00740134 Soprano Book/Online Audio $26.99
00740082 Mezzo-Soprano/Alto Book Only $17.99
00196404 Mezzo-Soprano/Alto Book/Online Audio $25.99
00740083 Tenor Book Only $16.99
00740136 Tenor Book/Online Audio $27.99
00740084 Baritone/Bass Book Only $17.99
00740137 Baritone/Bass Book/Online Audio $27.99

First 50 Broadway Songs You Should Sing

These collections of songs from the 21st century feature 33-37 songs per volume, with songs in original keys only, and a different song list for each voice type, with plot notes. Includes songs from Broadway, Off-Broadway and Off-Off Broadway.

00196404 High Voice $16.99
00196405 Low Voice $16.99

Girls' Songs from the 21st Century

These collections of songs from the 21st century feature 33-37 songs per volume, with songs in original keys only, and a different song list for each voice type, with plot notes. Includes songs from Broadway, Off-Broadway and Off-Off Broadway.

00287561 Book/Online Audio $17.99

Musical Theatre for Classical Singers

These collections of songs from the 21st century feature 33-37 songs per volume, with songs in original keys only, and a different song list for each voice type, with plot notes. Includes songs from Broadway, Off-Broadway and Off-Off Broadway.

00001224 Soprano Book Only $29.99
00230099 Soprano Book/Online Audio $44.99
00230000 Soprano 3 Accompaniment CDs $29.99
00001225 Mezzo-Soprano Book Only $29.99
00230100 Mezzo-Soprano Book/2 Accomp. CDs $44.99
00230101 Mezzo-Soprano 2 Accomp. CDs $29.99
00001226 Tenor Book Only $29.99
00230101 Tenor Book/2 Accompaniment CDs $44.99
00230002 Tenor 2 Accompaniment CDs $29.99
00001227 Baritone/Bass Book Only $29.99
00230102 Baritone/Bass Book/3 Accomp. CDs $44.99
00230003 Baritone/Bass 3 Accompaniment CDs $24.99

Musical Theatre Songs of the 2010s

An expansive selection of songs from new musicals and films from 2010-2019, representing hit productions like The Band's Visit, Dear Evan Hansen, A Gentleman's Guide to Love and Murder, Hamilton, The Lightning Thief, The Prom, Tootsie and more.

00299924 Women's Edition $29.99
00299925 Men's Edition.. $29.99

Theatre and Cabaret Comedy Songs

A collection of the funniest songs written for the state and screen. Features over 30 songs from classic and contemporary Broadway shows, and from songwriters Jeanine Tesori, Kerrigan and Lowdermilk, Goldrich and Heisler, Ryan Scott Oliver and more.

00194031 Women's Edition $24.99
00194032 Men's Edition.. $24.99

21st Century Musical Theatre

This series features 50 songs from dozens of shows, some that have never before appeared in any vocal collections. Includes songs from A Gentleman's Guide to Love & Murder; Hamilton; Kinky Boots; Wicked; and many more.

00262376 Women's Edition
.... $29.99
00130465 Men's Edition.. $29.99

HAL•LEONARD®
www.halleonard.com